UMRAH GUIDE BOOK

*In the Footsteps of the Prophets:
Understanding the Significance of
Umrah*

IDRIS ABU ANEESA

TABLE OF CONTENT

Introduction

Umrah, the lesser pilgrimage, is one of the most sacred and significant acts of worship in Islam. While not obligatory like Hajj, Umrah holds a special place in the hearts of Muslims, offering an opportunity to cleanse the soul, seek forgiveness, and draw closer to Allah. This sacred journey to the holy city of Mecca is a profound spiritual experience that leaves an indelible mark on the lives of those who undertake it.

The purpose of this guidebook is to provide a comprehensive and accessible resource for anyone preparing to perform Umrah. Whether you are a first-time pilgrim or someone returning to Mecca to renew your spiritual commitment, this guide will walk you through every step of the journey—from understanding the significance of Umrah and making the necessary preparations, to performing the rituals and reflecting on the experience afterward.

In the pages that follow, you will find detailed explanations of each ritual, practical advice on how to prepare for the journey, and spiritual insights to help you connect more deeply with the experience. We will explore the meaning behind the rites of Ihram, Tawaf, Sa'i, and more, offering you not just the "how" but also the "why" of each act of worship. Understanding the significance of these rituals will enhance your spiritual experience and allow you to perform them with greater mindfulness and devotion.

Umrah is more than just a physical journey; it is a journey of the heart and soul. It is a time for introspection, repentance, and renewal—a chance to leave behind the distractions of daily life and focus entirely on your relationship with Allah. By embarking on this sacred pilgrimage, you are following in the footsteps of countless believers who have sought the mercy and blessings of Allah in the holy city of Mecca.

This guidebook is designed to be your companion on this spiritual journey, providing you with the knowledge, tools, and inspiration you need to make your Umrah a deeply fulfilling and transformative experience. May Allah guide your steps, accept your efforts, and bless you with a successful and rewarding pilgrimage. Ameen.

1.1 What is Umrah?

Umrah is a pilgrimage to Mecca, Saudi Arabia, that can be undertaken at any time of the year, unlike the Hajj pilgrimage, which has specific dates in the Islamic lunar calendar. Although it is not obligatory like Hajj, Umrah holds significant spiritual value and is often referred to as the "lesser pilgrimage." The word "Umrah" in Arabic means "to visit a populated place," and in the context of Islam, it refers to visiting the holy sites in Mecca to perform specific religious rituals.

The primary rituals of Umrah include entering the state of Ihram (a sacred state), performing Tawaf (circumambulating the Kaaba), and Sa'i (walking between the hills of Safa and Marwah). These acts symbolize the unity of Muslims around the world in worshiping one God, and they serve as a means to seek forgiveness, purification, and spiritual rejuvenation.

1.2 Significance and Virtues of Umrah

Umrah holds immense significance in Islam. It is an opportunity for Muslims to cleanse their sins, seek Allah's mercy, and renew their commitment to their faith. The Prophet Muhammad (peace be upon him) emphasized the virtues of performing Umrah, saying, "The performance of Umrah is an expiation for the sins committed between it and the previous Umrah" (Sahih Bukhari).

Performing Umrah is also seen as a way to attain closeness to Allah. The rituals performed during Umrah are acts of worship that reflect a Muslim's devotion, humility, and obedience to Allah. The journey to Mecca and the performance of Umrah serve as a reminder of the temporary nature of this world and the importance of focusing on the hereafter.

Additionally, Umrah allows Muslims to experience a deep sense of unity and brotherhood with other believers. Pilgrims from diverse backgrounds come together in Mecca, dressed in the simple white garments of Ihram, erasing all distinctions of race, nationality, and social status. This sense of equality and fraternity is a powerful reminder of the universal message of Islam.

1.3 Difference Between Hajj and Umrah

While both Hajj and Umrah are pilgrimages to Mecca, there are several key differences between the two. One of the Five Pillars of Islam, the Hajj is a mandatory religious event that every Muslim who is financially and physically capable of performing should do at least once in their lives. Hajj takes place during the Islamic month of Dhu al-Hijjah, and its rituals are performed over specific days.

Umrah, on the other hand, is not obligatory but is highly recommended. With the exception of the Hajj days, it can be done at any time of year. The rituals of Umrah are fewer and less time-consuming than those of Hajj, making it a more accessible form of pilgrimage for many Muslims.

The primary difference in the rituals of Hajj and Umrah lies in the inclusion of additional rites in Hajj, such as the standing at Arafat (Wuquf), the stoning of the devil (Ramy al-Jamarat), and the sacrifice of an animal (Qurbani). Umrah, in contrast, focuses mainly on Tawaf, Sa'i, and the act of cutting or shaving the hair.

1.4 When to Perform Umrah

In contrast to Hajj, which has set dates, Umrah can be done year-round. However, many Muslims choose to perform Umrah during the holy month of Ramadan due to the increased spiritual rewards associated with it. "Performance of Umrah during Ramadan is equal to Hajj in reward," the Prophet Muhammad (peace be upon him) reportedly stated (Sahih Bukhari).

While Umrah can be performed year-round, certain times of the year may see higher numbers of pilgrims, such as during Ramadan, school holidays, or the period just before and after the Hajj season.

Pilgrims planning to perform Umrah should consider the potential crowds and weather conditions when choosing the timing of their pilgrimage.

1.5 Requirements and Eligibility for Umrah

Before embarking on the journey of Umrah, it is essential for pilgrims to understand the requirements and eligibility criteria. First and foremost, a Muslim intending to perform Umrah must be physically and financially capable of undertaking the journey. This includes being in good health, having the financial means to cover the cost of travel, accommodation, and other expenses, and ensuring that any financial obligations or debts are settled before departure.

A valid passport and an Umrah visa are required to enter Saudi Arabia for the purpose of performing Umrah. The visa can be obtained through authorized travel agencies or online platforms designated by the Saudi government. It is important to follow the visa application process carefully and provide all necessary documentation, including proof of vaccination, especially given the health regulations that may be in place due to ongoing global health concerns.

Additionally, women under the age of 45 are required to be accompanied by a Mahram (a male relative such as a husband, father, brother, or son) during the pilgrimage. However, some exceptions have been made in recent years, allowing women over a certain age to travel in groups without a Mahram, but this depends on specific visa regulations at the time.

Furthermore, pilgrims must also prepare themselves spiritually before embarking on Umrah. This includes making sincere intentions (Niyyah) for the pilgrimage, seeking forgiveness from those they may have wronged, and asking for Allah's forgiveness for their own sins. It is also recommended to study the rituals of Umrah in advance, ensuring that they are performed correctly and with full awareness of their significance.

In conclusion, Umrah is a profound spiritual journey that offers Muslims the chance to cleanse their souls, renew their faith, and seek closeness to Allah. Understanding the significance, timing, and requirements of Umrah is essential for those who wish to perform this sacred pilgrimage, ensuring that it is undertaken with the proper mindset and preparation.

Chapter 2:

Preparation for Umrah

Preparing for Umrah involves more than just packing your bags and booking a flight. It's a spiritual journey that requires thoughtful preparation in both mind and body. This chapter will guide you through the essential steps to ensure that your Umrah experience is fulfilling, meaningful, and smooth.

2.1 Spiritual Preparation

2.1.1 Intention (Niyyah) and Purity of Heart

The journey of Umrah begins with a pure heart and a sincere intention (Niyyah). In Islam, the intention behind any act of worship is crucial, and Umrah is no exception. Before embarking on this sacred journey, it is vital to cleanse your heart of any ill feelings, grudges, or worldly distractions. Umrah is not just a physical pilgrimage but a spiritual retreat that draws you closer to Allah. Reflect on why you are undertaking this journey and renew your intention to seek Allah's pleasure and forgiveness.

The Prophet Muhammad (peace be upon him) emphasized the importance of Niyyah in every action, saying, "Actions are but by intentions, and each man will have only what he intended" (Bukhari & Muslim). This Hadith underscores that the reward for Umrah is directly tied to the sincerity of your intention. Take time to engage in self-reflection and prayer, asking Allah to purify your heart and grant you the strength to perform Umrah with humility and devotion.

2.1.2 Understanding the Rituals

Before performing Umrah, it's essential to have a thorough understanding of the rituals involved. Each step of Umrah has deep spiritual significance, and performing them with awareness enhances the experience. Study the rituals of Umrah, including Ihram, Tawaf, Sa'i, and Halq or Taqsir. Familiarize yourself with the duas (supplications) recited at each stage, and practice them beforehand so that you can focus on worship rather than struggling to remember the words during the pilgrimage.

In addition to understanding the rituals, learn about the history and significance of the holy sites you will visit, such as the Kaaba, Safa and Marwah, and the Zamzam Well. This knowledge will deepen your connection to the pilgrimage and allow you to perform Umrah with a heightened sense of spirituality.

2.1.3 Dua (Supplication) for the Journey

Dua is a powerful tool for a believer, and it plays a crucial role in the journey of Umrah. Begin your journey with the supplication for travel, which the Prophet Muhammad (peace be upon him) used to recite: "O Allah, we ask You for goodness and piety in this journey of ours, and we ask You for actions that please You. O Allah, make this journey of ours easy for us and make its distance short. O Allah,

You are the Companion on the journey and the Guardian of the family" (Muslim).

Continue making dua throughout your journey, asking Allah for ease, acceptance of your Umrah, and protection from any harm. Supplicate for yourself, your family, and the entire Muslim ummah. Remember, Umrah is an opportunity to draw closer to Allah, and sincere supplication is a means to achieve this closeness.

2.2 Physical and Practical Preparation

2.2.1 Obtaining a Visa

Before you can embark on your Umrah journey, you must obtain an Umrah visa, which allows you to enter Saudi Arabia for the purpose of performing Umrah. The process of obtaining a visa varies depending on your country of residence, so it's essential to research the requirements well in advance.

Typically, you will need to apply through an authorized travel agency, which will handle the visa application on your behalf. The application process generally requires a valid passport with at least six months of validity remaining, recent passport-sized photographs, and proof of travel arrangements. Additionally, some countries may require a certificate of vaccination, particularly for meningitis. Ensure that you have all the necessary documentation ready and submit your application early to avoid any delays. Keep in mind that Umrah visas are usually issued only for a specific period, so plan your travel dates accordingly.

2.2.2 Travel Arrangements

Once your visa is secured, the next step is to arrange your travel to and from Saudi Arabia. Consider booking your flights well in advance, as prices can fluctuate significantly, especially during peak seasons such as Ramadan and the Hajj season. Direct flights to Jeddah or Madinah are ideal, as they minimize travel time and reduce the stress of layovers.

When selecting your accommodation, prioritize proximity to the Haram in Makkah and the Prophet's Mosque in Madinah. Staying close to these holy sites allows you to maximize your time in worship and minimizes the physical strain of walking long distances. Many hotels offer shuttle services to the Haram, which can be a convenient option if you are staying slightly farther away.

In addition to flights and accommodation, consider other logistics such as ground transportation. You may need to arrange for transportation between Jeddah, Makkah, and Madinah. Many travel agencies offer comprehensive packages that include flights, accommodation, and transportation, which can simplify the planning process.

2.2.3 Packing Essentials for Umrah

Packing for Umrah requires careful consideration to ensure that you have everything you need without overpacking. The following are some necessities to pack in your luggage:

- Ihram Garments: Men will need two pieces of white, unstitched cloth to wear as Ihram. Women can wear any modest clothing that meets the requirements of Hijab. It's advisable to bring an extra set of Ihram garments in case one gets dirty.
- Comfortable Footwear: You will be doing a lot of walking, so bring comfortable sandals or shoes that are easy to slip on and off. Make sure your footwear is compliant with the requirements of Ihram.
- Toiletries: Pack unscented toiletries, as the use of scented products is prohibited during Ihram. This includes soap, shampoo, toothpaste, and deodorant. Also, bring a small towel and a travel-sized bag for your toiletries.
- Prayer Mat and Compass: A lightweight prayer mat is useful for praying in open areas, and a compass can help you determine the direction of the Qibla when you are not at the Haram.
- Documents: Keep your passport, visa, and other important documents in a secure, easily accessible

place. Consider using a money belt or a small pouch that can be worn under your clothing for added security.

- Medication: Bring any prescription medications you need, along with a small first aid kit that includes basic supplies such as band-aids, pain relievers, and antiseptic wipes. If you have any chronic conditions, it's advisable to carry a doctor's note and a sufficient supply of medication.

- Snacks and Water: Although food and water are readily available, it's a good idea to carry some snacks and a refillable water bottle, especially during the journey.

Packing thoughtfully ensures that you are well-prepared and can focus on the spiritual aspects of Umrah without worrying about physical discomforts.

2.3 Financial Considerations

2.3.1 Budgeting for Umrah

Performing Umrah involves several costs, including airfare, accommodation, transportation, food, and other expenses. Creating a budget before you embark on your journey is essential to ensure that you have enough funds to cover all necessary expenses without financial strain.

Start by researching the average costs of flights, accommodation, and transportation for the time of year you plan to perform Umrah. Factor in the cost of the Umrah visa, travel insurance, and any additional fees charged by your travel agency. Be sure to include a buffer in your budget for unexpected expenses or emergencies.

It's also important to consider the cost of food and daily expenses. While there are many affordable dining options in Makkah and Madinah, it's wise to allocate a reasonable amount for meals, especially if you plan to eat at restaurants or purchase snacks.

Additionally, budgeting for souvenirs, charity, and other miscellaneous expenses is important. Many pilgrims choose to give to those in need during their journey, so setting aside some funds for sadaqah (charity) is a noble and rewarding practice.

2.3.2 Managing Expenses During the Journey

Managing your expenses during Umrah requires careful planning and discipline. It's easy to get caught up in the excitement of the journey and overspend, but staying within your budget will allow you to focus on the spiritual aspects of Umrah without financial worries.

One way to manage expenses is to carry a mix of cash and a credit or debit card. While most places in Makkah and Madinah accept cards, it's useful to have cash on hand for small purchases, tips, or places that do not accept cards. When using your card overseas, be aware of transaction fees and exchange fluctuations.

Set daily spending limits and track your expenses to avoid overspending. Consider using a budgeting app or a simple notebook to record your daily expenditures. This will help you stay within your budget and ensure that you have enough funds for the entire trip.

It's also advisable to avoid unnecessary purchases and focus on the essentials. While it's tempting to buy souvenirs and gifts, remember that the true reward of Umrah lies in the spiritual journey, not material possessions. Prioritize spending on things that will enhance your experience and bring you closer to Allah.

This chapter offers a comprehensive guide to preparing both spiritually and practically for Umrah. It covers everything from setting the right intention and understanding the rituals to managing finances and packing essentials, ensuring that pilgrims are well-prepared for this sacred journey.

Performing Umrah

Umrah is a spiritual journey that requires both preparation and devotion. In this chapter, we will walk through the essential steps and rituals of performing Umrah, ensuring that you are fully prepared to undertake this holy pilgrimage.

3.1 Entering the State of Ihram

3.1.1 What is Ihram?

Ihram is the sacred state a pilgrim enters before performing the rituals of Umrah. This state is both physical and spiritual, symbolizing purity, humility, and devotion. For men, Ihram consists of two unsewn white cloths: one to cover the lower body (Izar) and the other to drape over the shoulders (Rida). Women wear modest, plain clothing that covers their entire body except for their face and hands, avoiding any adornments or perfumes.

3.1.2 How to Wear Ihram

For men, wearing Ihram involves specific steps to ensure that the garments are properly secured. First, wrap the Izar around your waist, securing it with a belt if necessary. Ensure that it covers your navel and extends down to your ankles. Next, drape the Rida over your shoulders, ensuring it covers your upper body. Women should wear loose-fitting, simple clothing that fulfills the Islamic requirements for modesty. It is important to wear Ihram with the right intention, reflecting on the humility and equality that these garments represent.

3.1.3 Prohibitions During Ihram

Once in the state of Ihram, certain actions become prohibited for both men and women. These include:

- Cutting Hair or Nails: Any form of grooming, including cutting hair, trimming nails, or plucking eyebrows, is forbidden.
- Using Perfume: The use of any fragrant substances, including scented soaps and deodorants, is prohibited.
- Engaging in Marital Relations: Sexual relations and any behavior that may lead to them are not allowed.
- Hunting or Killing Animals: Pilgrims are prohibited from hunting or killing animals, even if they are pests or pose a nuisance.
- Wearing Sewn Clothing (for men): Men must avoid wearing any stitched clothing, including undergarments, socks, or shoes that cover the ankle.
- Covering the Head (for men) or Face (for women): Men should not cover their heads with hats or turbans, and women should avoid covering their faces unless in the presence of non-Mahram men.

Violating these prohibitions may require an expiation, such as offering a sacrifice, feeding the poor, or fasting.

3.2 The Rituals of Umrah

3.2.1 Tawaf (Circumambulation)

Tawaf is one of the central rituals of Umrah, involving the circumambulation of the Kaaba, the sacred structure located in the center of Masjid al-Haram. Pilgrims perform Tawaf by walking around the Kaaba seven times in a counterclockwise direction, starting from the corner of the Black Stone (Hajar al-Aswad).

Before beginning Tawaf, make the intention (Niyyah) in your heart, expressing your devotion to Allah and your desire to complete this ritual as an act of worship. As you walk, you may recite prayers, supplications, or simply reflect on the greatness of Allah. It is recommended to recite the following prayer upon reaching the Black Stone:

"Bismillah, Allahu Akbar, wa Lillahil Hamd"
(In the name of Allah, Allah is the Greatest, and praise be to Allah)

Each time you complete a circuit, you may try to touch or kiss the Black Stone. However, if the area is too crowded, you can simply raise your hand toward it and continue your Tawaf. After completing the seven circuits, it is Sunnah (recommended) to pray two Rak'ahs (units of prayer) behind Maqam Ibrahim, the station of Abraham, if possible.

3.2.2 Sa'i (Walking Between Safa and Marwah)

After completing Tawaf, pilgrims proceed to perform Sa'i, the ritual of walking between the hills of Safa and Marwah. This ritual commemorates the desperate search of Hajar (Hagar), the wife of Prophet Ibrahim (Abraham), for water for her son Isma'il (Ishmael). The well of Zamzam, which continues to provide water to pilgrims, was revealed to Hajar during this search.

Sa'i involves walking briskly between Safa and Marwah seven times. The journey begins at Safa, where you should make the intention (Niyyah) and recite the following prayer:

"Safa and Marwah are in fact two of Allah's symbols. So whoever makes Hajj to the House or performs Umrah, there is no blame upon him for walking between them. And Allah is grateful and

Knowing to anybody who offers good service."*
(Quran 2:158)

During the walk, you may recite prayers, supplications, or reflect on the trials of Hajar and the mercy of Allah. Men are encouraged to run between the two green markers on the path, while women should continue walking. The ritual is complete after reaching Marwah on the seventh circuit.

3.2.3 Halq or Taqsir (Shaving or Trimming Hair)

The final ritual of Umrah is Halq (shaving the head) for men or Taqsir (trimming a portion of the hair) for both men and women. Shaving the head is considered more virtuous for men, but trimming is also acceptable. Women should trim a small portion of their hair, approximately the length of a fingertip, as a symbol of humility and submission to Allah.

After completing Halq or Taqsir, you are officially out of the state of Ihram, and all the prohibitions of Ihram are lifted. This marks the completion of Umrah, and you may now enjoy the blessings of being in the holy city of Makkah.

3.3 Visiting the Holy Sites

While performing Umrah, pilgrims have the opportunity to visit several sacred sites within Masjid al-Haram and its vicinity. These visits deepen the spiritual experience and allow pilgrims to connect with the rich history of Islam.

3.3.1 Masjid al-Haram

Masjid al-Haram, also known as the Grand Mosque, is the most sacred mosque in Islam. It is the focal point of Umrah, as it houses the Kaaba, the direction toward which Muslims around the world pray. The mosque is vast and can accommodate millions of worshippers, offering a profound sense of unity and devotion.

Pilgrims often spend time in Masjid al-Haram praying, reading Quran, and reflecting on the significance of their journey. The mosque is open 24 hours a day, allowing pilgrims to visit at any time, day or night. The serenity and spirituality of this sacred space are unparalleled, providing a unique opportunity for worship and reflection.

3.3.2 Kaaba

The Kaaba, a cube-shaped structure draped in a black cloth known as the Kiswah, is the most revered site in Islam. It is believed to have been built by Prophet Ibrahim and his son Isma'il as a house of worship dedicated to the one true God, Allah. The Kaaba is the focal point of Tawaf and the Qibla (direction of prayer) for Muslims worldwide.

Touching or kissing the Black Stone (Hajar al-Aswad) embedded in one corner of the Kaaba is a highly recommended act, symbolizing the connection between the pilgrim and the Prophet Muhammad, who placed the stone during the reconstruction of the Kaaba. However, due to the crowds, it is not always possible to do so, and pilgrims are encouraged to make a gesture toward the stone instead.

3.3.3 Maqam Ibrahim

Maqam Ibrahim, the Station of Abraham, is a glass enclosure near the Kaaba that houses a stone bearing the footprints of Prophet Ibrahim. It is believed that these footprints were left when Prophet Ibrahim stood on the stone while constructing the Kaaba. Pilgrims often pray two Rak'ahs behind Maqam Ibrahim after completing Tawaf, as recommended by the Prophet Muhammad.

3.3.4 Zamzam Well

The well of Zamzam, located within Masjid al-Haram, is a miraculous source of water that has provided sustenance to pilgrims for thousands of years. According to Islamic tradition, the well was revealed to Hajar and Isma'il by the Angel Jibreel (Gabriel) during their search for water in the desert. The water of Zamzam is considered pure and blessed, and pilgrims are encouraged to drink from it and take some back home as a souvenir.

Conclusion

Performing Umrah is a deeply spiritual and transformative experience. Each step of the pilgrimage, from entering the state of Ihram to completing the final rituals, is imbued with meaning and significance. By understanding the rituals and their importance, pilgrims can perform Umrah with greater devotion and reverence, fully appreciating the blessings of this sacred journey.

Chapter 4

After Umrah

Completing the sacred pilgrimage of Umrah is a deeply transformative experience for many Muslims. As the rituals conclude and the journey nears its end, the spiritual journey continues in the heart and mind of the pilgrim. This chapter explores the steps that follow the physical completion of Umrah, focusing on reflection, ongoing spiritual growth, and sharing the experience with others.

4.1 Reflecting on the Experience

4.1.1 Gratitude and Thankfulness

The moment you complete Umrah, it is essential to take time to reflect on the entire journey—both physically and spiritually. The act of Umrah is a profound experience that embodies submission, devotion, and a connection with Allah. As you reflect, one of the first feelings to embrace is gratitude. Gratitude is not only an acknowledgment of the successful completion of the pilgrimage but also a recognition of the blessings that made the journey possible.

Offer thanks to Allah for granting you the ability to perform Umrah, for the health, wealth, and time that made it feasible. Remember to also express gratitude for the guidance and support you received from family, friends, and fellow pilgrims. This gratitude can be expressed through dua (supplication), and it is recommended to pray for the continued strength to maintain the spiritual benefits gained during Umrah.

4.1.2 Spiritual Growth and Lessons Learned

Umrah is more than a series of rituals; it is a journey of the soul. The experiences during Umrah often bring about significant spiritual growth. As you look back, consider the lessons learned throughout the pilgrimage. Perhaps you discovered a deeper sense of patience while waiting in long queues or a stronger reliance on Allah during moments of physical exhaustion. These lessons are not to be left behind in the holy cities of Mecca and Medina but should be carried forward into your daily life.

Journaling can be a helpful tool for reflection. Writing down your thoughts, feelings, and experiences can help solidify the lessons learned and serve as a reminder of your spiritual journey long after you have returned home. Reflect on the emotions you felt during Tawaf, the awe-inspiring sight of the Kaaba, and the humility experienced during Sa'i. These reflections will not only reinforce the spiritual lessons but will also deepen your connection with Allah.

4.2 Continuing the Journey of Faith

4.2.1 Maintaining the Spiritual High

One of the challenges many pilgrims face after completing Umrah is maintaining the spiritual high they experienced during the pilgrimage. The serene environment of the holy cities, surrounded by fellow believers, creates a unique atmosphere that fosters a deep connection with Allah. However, returning to daily life, with its distractions and challenges, can make it difficult to maintain that same level of spiritual awareness.

To continue your spiritual growth, it is crucial to establish regular practices that keep the lessons of Umrah alive in your heart. Daily prayers, reading the Quran, and engaging in frequent dhikr (remembrance of Allah) are vital practices that help maintain the spiritual high. Additionally, setting aside time for personal reflection and continuing the habits developed during Umrah, such as increased charity and kindness, can keep the spiritual flame burning.

Another effective way to maintain your spiritual high is by staying connected with fellow pilgrims. Sharing your experiences, discussing the lessons learned, and supporting each other in maintaining the spiritual gains of Umrah can provide a strong sense of community and accountability. Whether through regular meetings, online forums, or social media groups, staying connected with like-minded individuals who understand the significance of your journey can be a powerful tool in preserving your spiritual growth.

4.2.2 Incorporating Rituals into Daily Life

The rituals of Umrah, though specific to the pilgrimage, hold valuable lessons that can be incorporated into everyday life. Tawaf, for example, is a physical act of circling the Kaaba, but it also symbolizes the centrality of Allah in a Muslim's life. Even after returning from Umrah, strive to keep Allah at the center of your life, just as you circled the Kaaba with devotion and focus.

Sa'i, the walking between the hills of Safa and Marwah, represents the perseverance and patience of Hagar (Hajar) in her search for water for her son,

Ismail. This act is a reminder of the importance of patience and reliance on Allah in times of difficulty. When faced with challenges in daily life, recall the determination of Hagar and seek to embody her perseverance.

Incorporating these lessons into your daily routine can strengthen your faith and keep the spirit of Umrah alive. Whether it's starting your day with a few moments of dhikr or making a conscious effort to help those in need, these small acts of devotion can have a significant impact on your spiritual journey.

4.3 Sharing the Experience

4.3.1 Inspiring Others to Perform Umrah

Your experience of Umrah is not only a personal journey but also a potential source of inspiration for others. Sharing your story can encourage and motivate those who have yet to undertake the pilgrimage. Whether through personal conversations, social media, or community events, talking about your Umrah journey can help others understand the significance and beauty of this sacred act.

When sharing your experience, focus on the spiritual aspects and the lessons learned rather than just the logistical details. Discuss how the journey deepened your connection with Allah, the moments of spiritual awakening, and the feelings of peace and fulfillment. By emphasizing the spiritual transformation, you can inspire others to seek the same connection with Allah through their own pilgrimage.

Additionally, consider organizing or participating in informational sessions or workshops for those planning to perform Umrah. Sharing practical tips, advice, and personal anecdotes can help future pilgrims prepare for their journey and approach it with the right mindset. Your firsthand experience can be invaluable in guiding others through the process and helping them avoid common pitfalls.

4.3.2 Documenting and Sharing the Journey

Documenting your Umrah journey is another way to preserve and share the experience. Whether through writing, photography, or video, capturing the moments of your pilgrimage can serve as a lasting reminder of the spiritual journey you undertook. These documents can be a source of inspiration not only for yourself but also for others who may read, view, or watch them.

Writing a detailed account of your Umrah experience can be particularly powerful. Start with the preparation phase, detailing your intentions, challenges, and the emotions you felt as you embarked on the journey. Describe the rituals, the spiritual high points, and the moments of reflection. Conclude with your return home and the ways in which the pilgrimage has impacted your daily life.

Photography and video can also be powerful tools for sharing your journey. Capturing the serene beauty of the holy sites, the unity of the Ummah (Muslim community) during Tawaf, and the personal moments of prayer and reflection can convey the essence of Umrah in a way that words alone cannot. When sharing these visuals, consider pairing them with reflections or insights to provide context and depth.

If you're comfortable, consider sharing your documentation with a broader audience. Social media platforms, blogs, or community newsletters can be effective ways to reach others who may be considering Umrah. By sharing your journey, you contribute to the collective understanding of Umrah and help others prepare for their own spiritual journey.

Conclusion

The journey of Umrah does not end with the completion of its rituals; it is a continuous process of spiritual growth and reflection. By taking the time to reflect on your experience, maintaining the spiritual high, and sharing your journey with others, you keep the spirit of Umrah alive in your heart and life. The lessons learned and the connection with Allah forged during Umrah can serve as a guiding light as you navigate the challenges and blessings of everyday life. As you return to your daily routine, remember that the essence of Umrah lies not in the physical acts alone, but in the spiritual transformation they inspire.

This chapter provides a comprehensive guide on how to internalize and sustain the spiritual benefits of Umrah after completing the pilgrimage.

Conclusion

As you reach the end of this Umrah guide, it's essential to reflect on the profound spiritual journey that Umrah represents. The pilgrimage to the holy city of Mecca is not merely a physical act; it is a deeply transformative experience that leaves an indelible mark on the heart and soul of every pilgrim. In this conclusion, we will revisit the spiritual significance of Umrah, discuss the long-lasting impact it has on a Muslim's life, and offer encouragement for future pilgrimages.

Recapping the Spiritual Significance of Umrah

Known as the "lesser pilgrimage," Umrah is deeply ingrained in the hearts of Muslims worldwide.

Unlike Hajj, which is obligatory once in a lifetime for those who are physically and financially able, Umrah is a voluntary act of worship that can be performed at any time of the year. Despite its voluntary nature, Umrah is a highly recommended and meritorious act that brings immense rewards and spiritual purification.

The journey of Umrah begins with the intention (niyyah) and the donning of the Ihram, a simple white garment that symbolizes purity, humility, and the unity of all Muslims. The Ihram serves as a reminder that in the eyes of Allah, all believers are equal, regardless of their social status, wealth, or nationality. This sense of unity is further reinforced during the Tawaf, as pilgrims from all corners of the globe circumambulate the Kaaba together in worship of the One true God.

The rituals of Umrah, including Tawaf, Sa'i, and the shaving or trimming of the hair, are not merely physical acts but are imbued with deep spiritual meaning. Tawaf represents the eternal bond between the Creator and His creation, while Sa'i commemorates the unwavering faith and perseverance of Hajar, the wife of Prophet Ibrahim (peace be upon him). The act of shaving or trimming the hair symbolizes the pilgrim's purification and the shedding of worldly attachments.

Throughout these rituals, the pilgrim is in a state of heightened awareness, constantly engaging in supplication, remembrance of Allah (dhikr), and seeking forgiveness for past sins. This spiritual journey culminates in a profound sense of closeness to Allah and a renewed commitment to living a life of piety, righteousness, and obedience to His commands.

The Long-Lasting Impact of Umrah

The completion of Umrah is not the end of the journey but rather the beginning of a new chapter in a Muslim's life. The experiences and lessons learned during Umrah have a lasting impact that extends far beyond the pilgrimage itself.

One of the most significant effects of Umrah is the sense of spiritual renewal it brings. Pilgrims often return home with a purified heart, free from the burdens of past sins and filled with a renewed sense of purpose. This spiritual rejuvenation serves as a powerful motivation to continue striving for righteousness in daily life. It encourages pilgrims to maintain the habits of worship and devotion that were cultivated during Umrah, such as regular prayer, fasting, and charitable giving.

Moreover, Umrah fosters a deep sense of humility and gratitude. The experience of standing before the Kaaba, surrounded by millions of fellow believers, reminds the pilgrim of their smallness in the grand scheme of creation. This humility leads to a greater appreciation of Allah's blessings and a stronger desire to serve others. Pilgrims often return home with a heightened awareness of the needs of those around them and a renewed commitment to helping those in need.

Umrah also strengthens the bonds of brotherhood and sisterhood within the global Muslim community. The pilgrimage provides an opportunity to meet and interact with Muslims from diverse backgrounds, fostering a sense of unity and solidarity. This sense of global brotherhood is a powerful reminder that the Muslim ummah is one body, united in faith and purpose.

Encouragement for Future Pilgrimages

While Umrah is a deeply fulfilling spiritual journey, it is important to remember that the path of a believer is a continuous one. The experiences and lessons gained from Umrah should inspire a lifelong commitment to spiritual growth and the pursuit of Allah's pleasure.

For those who have completed Umrah, it is highly encouraged to perform the pilgrimage again if circumstances allow. Each visit to the holy city of Mecca brings new insights, deeper reflections, and a greater sense of closeness to Allah. Repeating Umrah allows the believer to continually cleanse their soul, renew their faith, and seek forgiveness for any shortcomings.

For those who have yet to perform Umrah, this guide serves as an invitation to embark on this sacred journey. The rewards and blessings of Umrah are immense, and the experience is one that will remain etched in the heart for a lifetime. Whether you are a seasoned traveler or someone embarking on their first pilgrimage, know that the journey of

Umrah is a journey of love, devotion, and surrender to the will of Allah.

In addition to Umrah, Muslims are encouraged to strive towards the completion of Hajj, the greater pilgrimage. Hajj, which is one of the five pillars of Islam, is a once-in-a-lifetime obligation for those who are physically and financially able. The experience of Hajj is unparalleled in its significance and magnitude, and it is the ultimate act of worship for a Muslim.

Final Thoughts and Prayers for Pilgrims

As we conclude this guide, it is important to remember that the true essence of Umrah lies not in the outward rituals but in the sincerity of the heart. The ultimate goal of Umrah is to draw closer to Allah, seek His forgiveness, and earn His pleasure. This journey is one of self-purification, spiritual renewal, and a reaffirmation of faith.

To all the pilgrims who have undertaken or will undertake this blessed journey, I offer my heartfelt prayers. May Allah accept your Umrah, forgive your sins, and grant you the strength to continue on the path of righteousness. May He bless you with the opportunity to return to His house, the Kaaba, again and again, and may He grant you the ultimate reward of entering Paradise.

For those who are planning to perform Umrah, I pray that Allah makes your journey easy and grants you success in completing the pilgrimage with sincerity and devotion. May He protect you from harm, guide you in every step, and shower you with His infinite mercy and blessings.

In conclusion, the journey of Umrah is a journey of the heart. It is a journey that transcends time and place, connecting the believer with their Creator in a profound and intimate way. As you return to your daily life, carry with you the lessons, memories, and spiritual benefits of Umrah. Let this journey be a source of inspiration and guidance as you continue to navigate the challenges and opportunities of life.

May Allah grant us all the opportunity to perform Umrah and Hajj, and may He accept our efforts, forgive our shortcomings, and bless us with His eternal pleasure. Ameen.